what do we do with the bible?

RICHARD ROHR
what do we do with the bible?

Published in the United States of America in 2018
by the Center for Action and Contemplation,
Albuquerque, New Mexico

Published in Great Britain in 2019

Society for Promoting Christian Knowledge
36 Causton Street
London SW1P 4ST
www.spck.org.uk

Unless otherwise stated, the author uses his own translation and/or
paraphrase of Scripture. He draws from a variety of English translations,
including the Jerusalem Bible (JB), New American Standard Bible
(NASB), New English Translation (NET), J. B. Phillips New Testament
(Phillips), Revised Standard Version (RSV), and *The Message*.
CAC's practice is to reference chapter and verse for scriptural sources,
but not to identify precise translations.

British Library Cataloguing-in-Publication Data
A catalogue record for this book is available from the British Library

ISBN 978–0–281–08321–3
eBook ISBN 978–0–281–08322–0

1 3 5 7 9 10 8 6 4 2

Printed in Great Britain by TJ International

eBook by Manila Typesetting Company

Produced on paper from sustainable forests

CONTENTS

INTRODUCTION

For all its inspiration, all its marvelous one-liners, all the lives it has changed forever, the Bible persists as a major problem for many people. Put in the hands of egocentric, unloving, or power-hungry people, or those who have never learned how to read spiritually inspired literature, it is almost always a disaster. History has now demonstrated this, century after century, so this is not an unwarranted, disrespectful, or biased conclusion. The burning of heretics, the Crusades, slavery, apartheid, and the dismissal and oppression of native peoples were all justified through the use of select Scripture quotes.

So you know where I am heading, right at the beginning, my general approach is *to change the seer and not to change the text.* Only *converted* people can be entrusted with inspired writings. They alone will operate in a *symbiotic* ("shared life") relationship with words and stories. They alone are unlikely to use the Bible as a personal power pack, a hammer, or a rationale for their bad behavior. Stay in prayerful dialogue with almost any spiritual text—even a problematic one— and it will almost always bear fruit.

There is no doubt the Bible will continue to be, and surely needs to be, the primary authoritative source for both Jews and Christians, even though both groups have historically tried to tame this wild beast in different ways, normally without fully realizing they were doing so. Catholics were so bothered by its many problems, especially in illiterate cultures, that they basically avoided reading the Bible for centuries. (Admittedly, this was easy because the printing press had not yet been invented.) Catholics and Orthodox Christians ended up operating as if someone had to have a degree in theology from their own tradition to be able to understand the word of God. Our Christian common sense tells us that just cannot be true. Access to God cannot be top-down. Ironically, it is the authors of the truly *subversive* Bible text itself that almost always prefer the bottom, the edge, the outsider, and the oppressed group, starting with the enslaved people of Israel. "Yahweh fought on their side and against the Egyptians," according to Exodus 14:25. We seem to have a very biased God.

Early in its history, our Jewish forebears created interpretive traditions like *midrash,* which tried to offer several spiritual levels of meaning for any single text, and they created the Talmud—Mishna and Gemara—which tried to present histories and commentaries of interpretation. This had the effect of somewhat democratizing Bible study, and also put

Scripture in the hands of communities of believers instead of just isolated academics.

This is similar to what many Latin American pastors began to do in the late twentieth century under the influence of liberation theology in what they called "base communities." The papacy had kept authoritative interpretation in the hands of the Roman Office, bishops, and priests, thus retaining a very limited perspective. This was probably inevitable when most of Europe was illiterate and still convinced of "the divine right" of kings and authority figures in general. But it also separated the Bible from its critical leavening function for the ordinary Christian. It kept the clergy falsely empowered—even though they often knew very little Scripture themselves.

Unknown to most post-Reformation Christians, early centuries of Christianity, through authoritative teachers like Origen, Cyril of Alexandria, Augustine, and Gregory the Great, already encouraged as many as seven "senses" of Scripture. The literal, historical, allegorical, moral, symbolic, eschatological (the trajectory this creates for history and growth), and "primordial" or archetypal (commonly agreed-upon symbolism) levels of a text were often given serious weight among scholars. These levels were gradually picked up by the ordinary Christian through Sunday preaching (as is still true today) and presumed to be normative by those who heard them.

These different senses of Scripture were sometimes compared to our human senses of hearing, seeing, tasting, smelling, and touching, which are five distinct ways of knowing the same thing, but in very different "languages." After both the Reformation and the Enlightenment, we reduced our ways of knowing to *one* for all practical purposes—the supposedly rational/literal/historical—and we have largely compacted and limited the Bible to this one single sense for several centuries now, in both its Catholic and Protestant

WHAT DO WE DO WITH THE BIBLE?

forms. Our bandwidth of spiritual access to the Bible was, consequently, severely narrowed, it seems to me—and, as many would say, to the least spiritually helpful level. That something supposedly happened in one exact way, in one moment of time, does not, of itself, transfer the experience to *me,* or *us.* (I believe that such transformation is precisely the function of any spiritual text—or it is not a spiritual text or, at least, a spiritually broadening text. It is dead weight.)

Such a narrow approach largely creates an antiquarian society that prefers to look backward instead of forward. In my experience, it creates *transactional* religion much more than *transformational* spirituality. It idealizes individual conformity and group belonging over love, service, or actual change of heart.

Literalism was discredited from the beginning of the New Testament through the inclusion of four Gospel accounts of the same Jesus event, which hardly ever totally agree. Which is the "inerrant" one?

This issue arises even earlier. The first five books of the Bible—which constitute the Pentateuch—are thought to be, by most scholars, a compilation of at least four distinct sources. These four sources are normally called the Yahwist, the Elohist, the Deuteronomic, and the Priestly. They are often repetitive, different in style, and with many seeming contradictions that force us to recognize they were written by different authors and taken from different primary sources in very different periods of Jewish history. Which one is the most "inspired"? Which one is "true"?

The earlier centuries of Christianity were, of course, much closer to the trans-rational world of Jesus and his storytelling style of teaching (which does not lend itself to dogmatic or systematic theology). The Gospel says, "He would never speak to them except in parables" (see Matthew 13:34). The indirect, metaphorical, symbolic language of a story or parable seems to be Jesus' strongly preferred way of teaching spiritual realities. One Protestant scholar goes so far as to say that Jesus' use of Scripture is largely "allusive, paraphrastic, and—so far as it can be ascertained—eclectic."[1] Wow!

In other words, Jesus clearly picks and chooses from his own Scriptures and his interpretations are not usually completely literal, which I will document shortly. Once we lost such humility—and creativity—around words, especially after the Enlightenment, we did not even allow or hear this indirect style of teaching in Jesus—even though it is rather obvious throughout. (Are you really a sheep, a goat, or a flock? Is the Reign of God really a mustard seed?) We confused right-in-front of-us reality with symbolic words about reality, which left us some distance away from immediate experience. I believe this led to the postmodern revolt against religion in general and Bible quoters in particular. Basically, more and more people studied Literature 101 and learned how writing works!

8

They learned the difference between poetry, prose, novels, history, commentary, journalism, fiction, and nonfiction. They discovered that so-called "historical novels" were still historical, and that nonfiction included many ways of telling the truth.

Most non-writers (and untrained readers) failed to recognize the need to "tell all the truth but tell it slant,"[2] as Emily Dickinson (1830–1886) advised—and thus we lost the ability to teach deep truth in a spiritual way—which must maintain *its inherent mysteriousness and evocative nature.* Read the Apostle Paul's *Sermo Sapientia,* or sermon on wisdom, in 1 Corinthians 1:17–2:16, where he says that believers have an alternative way of knowing that prayerfully *contemplates a text* instead of using it as dualistic ammunition to protect our opinions or attack others.

I like Parker Palmer's recent description of contemplation as "any way one has of penetrating illusion and touching reality."[3] Instead, we ate voraciously of the dualistic "tree of the knowledge of good and evil," despite an early chapter of the Bible warning us never to do this—or we "would most surely die" (see Genesis 2:17). Our ability to let sacred texts penetrate our personal and cultural illusions has been considerably lessened ever since. Our recent history of legitimated slavery, apartheid, absurd wealth and economic disparity, torture, and unfettered capitalism suggests that we mostly used the Bible to maintain our illusions and for purposes of acquiring or maintaining power.

A non-contemplative reading of the Bible does not help us "touch reality" but instead creates self-serving ideologies. It tends to use the Bible to maintain its own egoic position, rather than to "penetrate illusion" as Palmer suggests. The contemplative mind implies some non-identification with the self, which Jesus calls "losing the self"—and thus finding the True Self.[4] Wisdom can only be had by *the non-dominating self,* knowing reality "center to center" and "subject to subject," *never dominating subject to dominated object,* which tends to be the Western way of knowing things.

Paul also set us on this *alternative intelligence* path by his early use of archetypal meanings and typologies, which he directly says he is doing in several places (see Romans 5:14 and 1 Corinthians 10:6; the author of Hebrews does the same throughout the letter, as does the author of the book of Revelation). Here everything is interpreted as a sign, type, or symbol for something else, which certainly does carry the dangers of incoherence or even irrelevance (as many of us experience in reading the book of Revelation). Nevertheless, the pre-Enlightenment mind was much more risk-taking, soulful, and imaginative ("spiritual"?) than literalists are today. It understood the power of symbol and metaphor to circle around any spiritual idea from many sides. Almost all of Jesus' parables begin with the exact same phrase: "The Reign of God *is like* . . ." Jesus fully knows he is speaking in metaphor, simile, story, and symbol. We do not grant him that freedom in recent centuries and thus we miss or avoid many of his major messages. We are much the poorer for it.

Of course, the mind already operates this way in our early childhood, while poets and good novelists do it for a living. What I hope to say here is that we must now learn to interpret *spiritual things in a spiritual way,* with a *stated methodology and some spiritual intelligence,* or we will no longer be taken seriously by our cultures or by serious minds and seekers—plus we, ourselves, will lack deep conviction, or what I call inner authority. People who rely only upon their *private and yet external authority source* are incapable of being dialogue partners with anybody who does not already agree with those authorities and their sources. Soon we spend most of our time selling the medium itself (Bible, Sacraments, denominations, ordination) and never get to the actual message. This is no exaggeration but, in fact, quite common.

Could this be the reason behind the vacuous and repetitive nature of so much preaching? Both the preachers and their audiences are doomed to remain in very small circles of culturally like-minded people. Their Jesus will never be a "Savior of the world" (see John 4:42) because they do not know how to talk to any world but their own. There seems to be a hidden assumption that "you must agree to my hidden assumptions before I can talk to you"! Such preachers and teachers do not know how to be "all things to all people," as Paul desires to be (see 1 Corinthians 9:19–23). Somehow Paul knew how to be a universal brother, just like Jesus, although he has not usually been seen that way. I would like to change that perception if I can.

An honest methodology of interpretation is especially needed for preachers and teachers, and for any who want to be taken seriously by non-believers. "Go out to the whole world and preach the good news to *all creation*" (see Mark 16:15) would seem to imply talking *to others* and not insisting that others fully agree with our predefined terms before we can talk to them. Where have we seen such enforced "belief" or interpretation work anyway? We cannot mandate such things as faith, hope, and love. If we try, we end up with civil religion (as we have had in much of history) and little real spirituality, or very passive-aggressive, quiet non-cooperation, as I see in many of our native peoples here in New Mexico and in many Catholic Sunday congregations. Basically, if we are not positively *excited* about our religion, it does not work for us in any meaningful way. Such positive excitement is its very function, you might say.

HERMENEUTIC

The word for a person's methodology or pattern of interpreting a spiritual text is called a hermeneutic. (This comes from the Greek words for "interpretation" and "art form".) If you prefer to just speak of your "science of interpreting" a text, that is fine; but if you are wise and want to create an intelligent spiritual following, you must show your cards and declare your policy and plan (your de facto hermeneutic) up-front. Most preachers, frankly, do not, although an attuned crowd does pick up a speaker's hermeneutic while listening to him or her over time—and they tend to unconsciously absorb it as the norm or the ideal. They soon pick their preferred preacher, who reflects their same set of biases—while not recognizing them as biases at all. This is true for both liberals and conservatives.

If you are any kind of teacher, you will do best *(even for yourself!)* if you develop and fully *own* your own operative hermeneutic, and eventually state it publicly, or people rightly conclude these are nothing more than your opinions, biases, fanciful ideas, and your own culture speaking. Then they will dismiss you just as easily. You must somehow be able to communicate that "it is not just you who are speaking, but the Spirit of God who is speaking through you" (see Matthew 10:20), as Jesus tells the first missionaries. I hope I can give you some helpful guidelines in this short book.

Unless we are drawing from the common and deep well of the shared Holy Spirit, why should anyone listen to us or trust us? They should ask of us what the scribes and teachers of the Law often asked of Jesus: "By what authority do you … ?" (see Mark 11:28). We must be prepared to somehow state our method of interpretation, including our conscious biases, or we end up being dishonest or manipulative with the text— without even knowing it. If we are clear, then, if people want to reject our message, that is their business.

We must somehow both give authority to the text (faith) and not let that authority get in the way of good critical thinking (understanding). Remember, Jesus does tell us to love God "with our whole mind" too (see Matthew 22:37). St. Anselm (1033/4–1109) defined theology as "faith seeking an understanding of itself" (*fides quaerens intellectum*). Our hermeneutic must make use of *both* our will and our intellect. Mere conformity (will) or mere reason (understanding) is always a dead faith, and unworthy of the full human person. (In general, people who call themselves conservative make faith largely a matter of conformity/will and those who call themselves liberal make faith largely a matter of reasonableness/intellect.)

What I hope to provide here are some training wheels that will have an inherent stability, are consistent with reality, and can be understood by the ordinary, good-willed person ("in the Spirit"), whether liberal or conservative. Our science of interpretation should not demand a theological, or even university, education. For persons in the Spirit (not pious, but *whole, and thus holy),* a spiritual text must be allowed to *simultaneously console and challenge both their individual ego and their group ego.* That is simply how healthy and well-disposed people grow and learn—by continuous boxing matches with their own shadow.

If a text largely appeals to the shadow self— triggering responses like self-serving anger, fear, exclusivity, punitiveness, superiority, or separateness—I assume it is not in the Spirit and is not Christian common sense—or even

18

good sense—but its opposite. Good scriptural interpretation does demand some initial surrender—an initial, goodwill act of faith—that then also needs understanding of itself (*fides quaerens intellectum*) if we are to appeal to the whole and mature person. Our hermeneutic is always going to demand a primary positive disposition (we normally cannot start with cynicism or skepticism, although some saints, like Paul and Augustine, have begun there and then moved beyond it). Then, however, we must also be encouraged to ask *why, how,* and *what,* with our trained intellect—so that the mind is not left dangling in a noose. God desires a love affair with persons, not an entanglement with robots.

THE PERENNIAL TRADITION

Most teachers of Eastern religions use the word "lineage" to communicate that their teaching is not just their private idea, but a part of an authoritative tradition and trajectory. They publicly own that they are buying into an accountable wisdom tradition larger than themselves, which many of us call the Perennial Tradition. This is quite similar to what the legal system calls "case law," where previous rulings by a court must guide any future rulings.

Wise people know their wisdom is not self-generated. It comes from a larger and deeper Source, which is always shared (some psychologists call this the collective unconscious and Christians call it the Holy Spirit). Most Buddhists are quite up-front about this, whereas most Christians just declare their chosen denomination, which really does not answer the question. Our de facto hermeneutic tends to be self-constructed over time—and not just from the group to which we belong. It is a combination of our cultural group think, our precise education, and our recognized personal biases.

Do know that *there is no such thing* as *a bias-free position.* That is the illusion and always-present lens that Martin Luther (1483–1546) failed to notice when he shouted, "*sola Scriptura!*" ("only Scripture!"). The same is true for Catholics, who usually relied on their own smaller, local traditions, which they absolutized, often knowing little about the Great Tradition that included native religions, Judaism, and the Eastern Church, which we largely ignored after the Great Schism of 1054. This made them not really "catholic" (universal) at all, but largely Roman and Western European. Be careful when anybody says "only." It is a giveaway for narrow-gauge and dualistic thinking. We must recognize that we all have our own filters and lenses. They are completely "wrong" only when they are not recognized. Think about that.

I would declare my own tradition or lineage to be the Perennial Tradition, specifically in light of the *whole* history of the

Catholic Christian Tradition, which builds on natural religion.[5] This is my constant source and desire and, also, my up-front and owned bias. Further, my theological bias is "a bias toward the bottom," which I learned from the prophets, Jesus, Francis of Assisi, Thérèse of Lisieux, and liberation theology. I am so convicted of this bias that I have an inherent mistrust of any enlightenment, holiness, or salvation theory that does not lead a person to a love and protection of the marginalized ones, the outsider, the sinner, the so-called unworthy ones, the earth beneath our feet, or what Jesus calls "the least of the brothers and sisters" (see Matthew 25:31–46).This normally corrects any attempt to use our spirituality as a superiority game or elitist worldview. How we treat the vulnerable and powerless among us tends to reveal the real operative agenda of any person or culture.

Finally, my personality bias (for good and for ill) is that I tend to be far too serious, zealous, and idealistic, which was revealed to me through my Enneagram typology as a "One." My compulsive way of seeing is also my very best way of seeing, when I can be very clear, focused, and determined toward the good. You need to recognize the depth and breadth of your own set of blinders, and enjoy your unique binoculars! Just remember, your gift is the flip side of your "sin" and your sin is the dangerous side of your gift. You must accept and recognize *both*, which will always keep you both humble and wise.[6]

All of these filters will give you a pretty good indicator of how I personally will interpret my reality or any text. Then you can choose to agree or not agree, but at least you know what you are accepting or rejecting. Of course, you must recognize your own biases too because biases are largely hidden assumptions that are fully taken for granted. This is often how a good spiritual director or therapist can help you in facing your shadow issues. I get some of my strongest pushback, for example, when I dare to criticize capitalism in any way (even more than race or gender!). This would seem to reveal the depth—and hiddenness—of one very unquestioned bias in America. When you cannot see it as a bias, that is precisely when it is most operative—and why we say it is hidden in the "shadows."

If you do not make your own interpretive biases conscious and shareable, you will be able to argue in whatever direction your ego or the cultural mood deems helpful in the moment. The most common default position for Scriptural interpretation is, of course, the literal/historical one—which is honestly the least helpful and the least fruitful. It takes neither courage nor creative imagination, but merely the endless and useless arguments of, "Did this really happen in exactly this way?" and "Do I have to believe that it happened in just this way?" These questions are *largely a waste of time in terms of soul*

24

development. We have wasted much of the last several hundred years on such futile questions, even hating over them and dividing over them. Our very fear of sliding down a supposedly slippery slope seems to be the slippery slope itself.

ADOPTING ADDITIONAL LENSES

Yet, is this narrow lens—"Did it really happen in exactly this way?"—not the focus of most preaching we have heard? It tends to reflect and mirror our own era and local culture and thus cannot really challenge that culture. It tends to mirror the ego's current prejudices and thus cannot really change them. I would have to say that *culturally bound* preaching is the general norm. It is also probably the major reason why our secular society does not take Bible quoters very seriously, and why Christians do not call forth any real alternative society. Secular society, rightly or wrongly, now assumes, for example, that Southern Evangelicals are racist and classist, while northeastern Catholics are heady and secular, because that appears to have been their general bias up to now. They are not considered objective and thus can only create tribes instead of transformed people. We lose spiritual authority when our preaching just bounces around inside of a local hall of mirrors.

Luther was trying to bring some much-needed critical thinking to overly mythological Catholicism in the sixteenth century, but his uncritical pendulum swing also sent us down a rabbit hole that has seriously narrowed our field of vision to this day. We now call it "fundamentalism." The Reformation's critical thinking was surely a necessary stage in our maturation process—but we cannot permanently rest in oppositional thinking. We must continue toward mystical, non-dual, and conciliatory patterns. The overreaction that produced fundamentalism soon set in motion an equal and opposite reaction called rationalism. This is the present argumentative frame inside of which we are trapped. There must be some good alternatives and subtleties to this false dualistic split between non-critical fundamentalism and overly critical rationalism.

PROBLEMATIC TEXTS

Bothersome stories very often pull us into universal dilemmas, fill us with discontent, and drive us to a third and better alternative. If every Biblical story tied things together into a nice obvious lesson, like *Grimms' Fairy Tales*, it would not serve its function as a spiritual text. Such indirection and asymmetry appear to be the way the Bible and most storytellers teach! Such teaching creates the very problems that then beg for a better answer. The problem is stated and somehow included in the hopeful solution. This is the way that universal mythmakers teach.

Show me a good story that does not have a villain, a problem, an evil act. The trouble is that fundamentalists often use the regressive person or story to justify their own regressive behavior. It is not used as a goad to move beyond and forward by staying with and growing through the conflict, but as a subtle permission to stay the same. "Saul and David killed their enemies, so it must be okay." "Slavery is taken for granted in almost all of the Bible, so it can't be too bad."

The number of violent, dualistic, imperialistic, sexist, clannish, patriarchal, homophobic, fully contradictory, and historically entrapped texts in the Bible are just too many to be contradicted or roundly dismissed. Now, when anyone calls such a Bible "inerrant," most modern and postmodern people just discount the honesty or thoughtfulness of the speaker.

Good scriptural interpretation is not limited by the rational lens, but that does not mean it is irrational either. There is also the childlike lens of the pre-rational, the adult's intelligent reason, and the very sophisticated lens of the trans-rational, the symbolic, and the mystical. This last is our wide-angle and long-distance lens, which provides the basis for our Biblical hermeneutic. We need all three. In fact, I would correlate the pre-rational with the always unknowable work of the Creator, the rational with the visible work of Christ, and the trans-rational with the ubiquitous work of the Holy Spirit.

Without such a wide-angle lens, we create people who are largely argumentative (which is almost Christianity's brand name today) instead of peacemakers, healers, or builders. In fact, many will go so far as to say, "There is so little inspiring spiritual teaching in the Bible!" or ask, "Why do we need to know about all these wars, murders, rapes, horrible kings, deceits, and stories of such immature people for our bedtime reading?" The Bible appears to be mostly Jewish history and polemic, largely uninspiring except for the Psalms, some select stories, and most of the Gospels—yet even these are set in an entirely different culture, where we do not know the ground rules or the assumptions.

One sincere and intelligent seeker once asked me, "Why can't we just have a simple book like *Seven Habits for Highly Holy People*? This book is too filled with uninspiring, confusing, violent, and contradictory texts." I can see why a reasonable person could ask this, yet the Bible is not going to go away—and it does pull us into the blood and guts of real, historical life. Could that be much of its intended message? (By the way, other believers face very similar problems with the Koran, the Upanishads, the many legends surrounding the Buddha, and the unwritten sayings of most native religions, all of which can be totally misused for one's own purposes. We are all in this dilemma together.) Is there any way out of this?

INCARNATION

I do think God gave us a wonderful way out of this word-bound conundrum in the Gospel of John, where it States, "And the word became flesh and lived among us" (see 1:14). We Christians call this event the Incarnation (Enfleshment, Manifestation, Embodiment, or Epiphany all work too), which implies that God entered material reality from the very beginning (see Ephesians 1:3–14), and thus hides and reveals the Divinity in and through our physical universe. As Paul directly puts it, *Ever since the creation of the the invisible existence of God and the Divine Power can be clearly seen by the mind's understanding of created things*" (see Romans 1:20). These words undercut and self-correct the absolute and autonomous authority of Scripture—from the inside out! They base spiritual wisdom in nature, in creation, and from the beginning, thus preceding all later spiritual writings, which were composed in the last nanosecond of geologic time.

I call this the Universal Christ[7] and this is the foundational premise in my Biblical hermeneutic: Material reality, nature, precedes and grounds all words about spiritual things. We need to *just look* at reality in a contemplative way before we start verbalizing what it is that we think we are seeing. All verbalizations are, by definition, metaphors and never primary speech or primary seeing. A good definition of contemplative seeing is, "a long, loving look at the Real."[8] That most simple understanding is still hard to beat.

I was recently on a speaking tour that led me to many medieval churches in Germany and middle Europe. I was told that it was common in the Medieval sculptures and paintings of the Annunciation to have Mary dropping a book out of her hands at the same moment of Gabriel's proclamation, "You are to conceive in your womb" (see Luke 1:32). Soon I was seeing this almost unnoticed pattern again and again in German church art. Once we get the physical incarnation, or personal experience, the verbal falls away in its absolute importance and centrality. Once God is "conceived in our womb," as it were, all outer signifiers become secondary and, in some way, even unnecessary. That has to be true!

Now, with that as a long introduction, let's move our hermeneutic to an even more practical and specific level. Let me offer you some guidelines to help form your own spiritual way of reading the Bible.

WHAT THE BIBLE IS **NOT** SAYING

That there is only one inerrant way of communicating the truth.

This is clearly and directly taught by giving us *four* Gospel accounts of the same incidents, which usually differ considerably, sometimes on major points. For example, which account of Jesus' words at the Last Supper is the true/official one? Which leper story is false news and which one is authentic journalism?

We need to have "the very words" of Jesus—and others.

The entire New Testament is written in Greek, which we have no evidence that Jesus knew or spoke. We do not know exactly what he said, word for word, except perhaps the few times he is quoted with an Aramaic phrase.

If the exact words were important, Jesus would have appeared in the age of audio and video recordings. But he—and the whole Bible—risked God's message being remembered and passed on through the vagaries of oral tradition, repetition, and biased memory.

The Biblical words enter the world unmediated by human writers, human errors, and human limits.

Paul says quite directly that "the knowledge that we have now is imperfect" (see 1 Corinthians 13:12). Then Peter says of Paul, "In all his letters there are passages that are hard to understand, and these are the ones that uneducated and unbalanced people distort in the same way that they distort all of Scripture" (see 2 Peter 3:16). Internal course-correction, one might call it.

Then there are the manuscripts themselves. We see deletions or "corrections" in even the oldest known manuscripts. Why do we want to pretend that the Bible fell fully produced from heaven in a zip-top bag?

The Bible can be understood as isolated texts outside of any appropriate context.

Try this telling case (there are many more): "All Cretans are liars, dangerous animals, and lazy. This is a statement upon which you can rely" (see Titus 1:12–13). Is this an inspired text—even in its original context? This "proof text" approach to Scripture, which allows us to find a single line to prove or illustrate almost anything, has now been universally discredited and, also, shown to lead us to some very dangerous and difficult conclusions.

The Bible is inspired differently than God inspires anything else.

The Bible follows the universal pattern of divine inspiration. It evolved, like the ages and eras of the universe and planets themselves, through many stages of writing, redaction, rearrangement, many edits, and compilations. As I stated earlier, the four different, ancient sources of the Pentateuch—the Yahwist, the Elohist, the Deuteronomic, and the Priestly—developed at very different periods in history. What we know as the book of Genesis likely came together as late as 500 BC. We tried to understand a totally dynamic God through a very static notion of time and history.

We also know that Jewish, Catholic, and Protestant voting councils long argued and disagreed on the exact canon, which is why we still speak of the Apocrypha, the Deuterocanonicals, or the Secondary Canon. Most people frankly operate by giving more authority to some books than to others (John's Gospel over Joshua and Judges, Paul's letters to the Corinthians over the book of Revelation). Of course, we cannot say that publicly—although I just did. God sure took a lot of unnecessary risks. Maybe that heavenly zip-top bag would have been a good idea.

All the above make the Bible an uninspired and untrustworthy text.

Rather than conclude this, I would suggest we adjust our understanding of how God *in-spires* (from the Latin "to breathe") anything— from the created universe, to the written word, to the Body of Jesus, to bread and wine, to our own bodies. It is always based on faith insight and on a symbiotic relation-ship between the seer and *what meaning he or she is willing and able to see.* Inspirited people can and will almost naturally see inspira-tion in a text or a story. Blocked or devious people will merely use or manipulate a text, no matter how spiritual it is. The Bible does not demand academic scholarship, but it is indeed dangerous in the minds of unbalanced or agenda-driven people.

All visible or heard words are inhabited by an interior "inscape" that does not demand belief, but only invites response and participation. *A truly spiritual text can call forth both an in-depth response and a very childlike response, at the same time, and they do not need to contradict one another. In fact, they might need one another.* God never forces the Spirit on us. The Holy Spirit invites forward, softens, warms, and overcomes unnecessary dualisms. It never increases dualistic divides through anger, rash judgment, or misunderstanding. The Bible cannot force, nor will it ever be able to prove itself to be inspired. Inspiration is a shared event, a symbiotic relationship that we often call *faith* and sometimes call *presence.* Inspired people can best read inspired texts and keep them inspired. Uninspired people

40

literally suck the air out of everything. If you think this is just my dangerous idea, reread 1 Corinthians 2:14–16 and you will see it is Paul's dangerous idea too. I might add that it is Contemplation 101—*the seer determines what can or cannot be seen.*

HOW DID CHRISTIANS CREATE THE PROBLEM OF TEXT OUTSIDE OF CONTEXT?

This issue first developed, it seems to me, when we tried to understand Jesus while not understanding or appreciating that he was both Jewish and human. We extracted him from his own reality and made him a unique, one-time anomaly to be worshiped and praised. Context became unimportant and distracting. He was presented as the Archetypal Christ, above history, apart from the incarnate Jesus in history. But the Hebrew culture of Jesus' specific time and

41

place created the arena in which Jesus moved, built, reacted, and corrected. A non-Jewish Jesus is simply not Jesus. A nonhuman Jesus is simply not Jesus. When his divinity is allowed to totally trump his full humanity, we no longer have the authentic Manifestation or message; we have text without context, soul without embodiment, and, therefore, we no longer have any in-depth Gospel.

After AD 313, the message of Jesus was increasingly aligned with Empire in both the East and the West. In many ways, he and his message were rather fully co-opted to establish an agreed-upon state religion and to enforce compliance. There was no room for critical thinking, his clearly nonviolent thinking, or often even spiritual thinking. We needed and created a unifying God figure to be worshiped instead of a divine-human teacher to *be followed and imitated*. Very pointed teaching, where text and context are clearly linked, as we have in the Sermon on the Mount, was actually quoted less and less frequently in church documents. This Gospel message is far too clear and far too critical of our cultural idolatries of war, "storing up treasure," necessary enemies, and things as specific as taking oaths (see Matthew 5:34), upon which all false loyalty systems rely. The eight Beatitudes (Matthew 5:3–10), which are critical of all false power, were largely ignored in favor of the much more reliable Ten Commandments, which offered us the needed social order. The Beatitudes almost *encourage disorder*, with their weeping, longing, poverty, and the endurance of persecution. *Climbing cultures* have little use, appreciation, or even understanding of such things.

We also extracted Christ from the eternal love flow of the Trinity and made him into a lone male monarch, revealed as such in almost all language and art up to our own time. We henceforth understood the God relationship less in terms of a circle and flow of shared life, and more as a pyramid of feudal authority. Obedience and loyalty were the supreme virtues, not love and compassion—witness the Crusades, the Inquisition, burnings at the stake, and the anathemas and threats that ended most church councils until Vatican II. Top-down control and uniformity was the norm, even in many later Protestant groups, because it was the only way we could think in those times. We basically confused unity with uniformity until the last hundred years, and even now the difference is very slow in being understood.

Finally, for the first fifteen hundred years, until the invention of the printing press, the written message was unavailable to more than ninety-five percent of the Christian population, most of whom could not read or write. But once the written word was easily available, we fell in love with texts, not realizing that we usually had no context except our own through which to interpret them. In art, even images of the Holy Family were painted as Dutch or Italian citizens of their corresponding historical times. We pulled

Jesus into our context for immense incarnate good, but not for any critical thinking in terms of Amsterdam or Venice. Thus, we had neither context nor even authentic texts, but only accommodation and cultural narcissism.

WHO WERE THE INTERPRETERS?

During this time and, frankly, until the last few decades, the typical interpreters of the Bible were overwhelmingly educated males, often formally celibate, raised into a higher social class, and trained to broker and maintain an organized form of Christianity upon which their jobs depended. They often lived a more upper-class lifestyle, somewhere between nobility and peasants, probably the first real "upper middle class" in the West. (This culture that we call "clericalism" is what St. Francis and now Pope Francis are trying to reshape.) By not reading the Jewish prophets, except in terms of their "fore-telling" of Jesus, we failed to notice that the constant recipients of their ire and judgment are two special groups—the princes and the priests. Elitism, patriarchy, clericalism, and any attempt to create a privileged group of hearers is usually deemed highly dangerous in the Bible. Most of the prophets appear to have been "laypeople," as we understand the term, and not trained experts.

The view from the side of the peasants and the oppressed, so consistent in Jesus' lifestyle and parables (many of which con-trast landowners and workers), was largely lost. The socio-political context of the en-slaved and then colonized Hebrews, the crit-ical voice of the Jewish prophets, the un-derside worldview of Jesus, the working-class jobs of the twelve disciples, and Paul's tentmaking occupation were replaced in almost all cultures by a broad alignment with the dominant consciousness of money, war, and power. The radical-lifestyle message of Jesus no longer makes sense at this level—in fact, it starts sounding quite subversive.

So, we domesticated Christianity into a fast-food form that basically no longer necessitated an actual change of heart, mind, or social position. Lines like, "unless you change and become like children, you will never enter the Reign of God" (see Matthew 18:3) no longer made a bit of sense. The "eye of the needle," referenced in all three of the Synoptic Gospels (see Mark 10:25, Matthew 19:24, and Luke 18:25), was always located somewhere else and meant for someone else to navigate. We decided we could indeed serve both God and Mammon; never mind what Jesus said.

THE JESUS HERMENEUTIC

Given the above, even if you only par-
tially agree with what I have said, I can now
present to you what I think is a way of interpreting Scripture that is faith-filled, often
quite inspiring, self-critical (without which
all things become idolatrous), and also available to the ordinary person on the street,
with just some basic goodwill and what I
earlier called "spiritual common sense."

I promise you that this is anything but
an elitist, academic, or seminary-textbook
approach to the Bible. Here it is, in one
naive, straightforward line:

Let's use the Bible the way that Jesus did!

If that sounds like I am saying nothing, just know that is exactly what we have *not* done in most of our Christian history! (This is despite a common aphorism in most churches that said, "We understand the Old Testament in the light of Jesus.") In point of fact, we have largely ignored Jesus' pattern and style of using his own Jewish Scriptures. We often quoted many of his one-liners, but seldom imitated his underlying worldview or assumptions, or recognized his rather clear biases. When we watch his pattern of interpretation, we could even say Jesus "played light and easy" with the only Bible he knew—the Hebrew Bible. Jesus was anything but a fundamentalist or a legalist. This is not hard to demonstrate; in fact, it is culpable ignorance not to see it now.

Such constant daring is surely what got him killed by the priests, the scribes, and the teachers of the Law. After healing a sick man, Jesus says this to the Bible quoters of his day: "You pore over the Scriptures, believing that in them you have life, but now you have Life standing right in front of you, and you cannot recognize it!" (see John 5:39). Instead of recognizing with their own eyes the obvious good fruits of a healing, they constantly created pretexts (usually working on the Sabbath or acting like God) to hate and reject Jesus—who does fully identify with God (see John 5:18–19 and 10:30–38). Jesus is never hesitant to call himself, or allow himself to be called, God's "son." But we have not imitated him well in that regard. Instead, *we made Jesus into an exclusive child of God, rather than the inclusive model for all the rest of us, as sons and daughters too*—which, I believe, was his exact point!

Jesus largely ignores the Sabbath prohibition of work. We see him picking corn and both touching people and working with people rather regularly on Saturday, almost as if to flaunt this exaggerated, human-made law. But we now know that any pre-existent dislike of a person will always find its justification. According to Jesus, our eyes create what they want to see, and do not see what they do not want to see (e.g., Matthew 7:1–5). Jesus taught quite clearly on projection, denial, and reaction formation two thousand years before Freud, who thought he was the first to recognize these common defense mechanisms. This pattern has become overwhelmingly and sadly clear in the food fights of American partisan politics today.

We wanted Jesus for "orthodoxy" or *correct content* (that could then be mandated and compliance-enforced), but we thus lost sight of his *distinct process for getting us there*: his life stance; his recognition of social order, economy, and class as places to hide; his clear recognition of the disguises of the human shadow. These, of course, are much more threatening to the ego, so we tended to concentrate on the usual "hot sins," through which people could more easily be shamed and controlled. We soon made Jesus into

a purveyor of private rewards and punishments, inside a frame of mere retributive
justice—which was itself conveniently put
off until the next life. Delaying those rewards
and punishments kept us from basic self-
awareness and simple self-observation. I am
convinced that Jesus is presenting rewards
and punishments as inherent and present-
tense. Goodness is its own reward, evil its
own punishment. Humans seem to prefer
the zero-sum game of reward and punishment, in which our very "reward" is the
assurance of someone else's punishment—
or escape from our own. This does not create
great or loving people—at all.

JESUS' OTHER BIASES

Let me try to reveal the largely hidden
assumptions of the Jesus hermeneutic,
which led him to a truly very dangerous

approach to sacred texts. Here are some of the major ones:

* Relative to all the words recorded in the four Gospels, Jesus actually *does not quote Scripture that much*! In fact, he is criticized for not doing this: "You teach with [inner] authority and not like our own scribes" (see Mark 1:22).

* *Jesus talks much more out of his own experience of God and humanity* instead of teaching like the scribes and Pharisees, who operated out of their own form of *case law* by quoting previous sources. It is amazing that this did not give us more permission to do the same. This is probably what made him so edgy and dangerous to the religious establishment.

* Jesus often *uses what appear to be non-Jewish or non-canonical sources*, or at least sources we cannot verify. For example: "It is not the healthy who need the doctor, but the sick" (see Mark 2:17, Matthew 9:12, and Luke 5:31),

or the parable of the rich man and Lazarus (see Luke 16:19–31). His bandwidth of authority and attention is much wider than *sola Scriptura.* He even quotes some sources seemingly incorrectly (e.g., John 10:34)!

• Jesus himself *wrote nothing that persists.* He did not appear to want us to rely on his exact formulations. He knew the danger and legalism of "by the book" people. (St. Francis did not want to write a Rule for us Franciscans for the same reasons, but Rome forced him to do it.)

• Jesus *never once quotes from nineteen of the books in his own Scriptures.* In fact, he appears to use a very few favorites: Exodus, Deuteronomy, Isaiah, Hosea, and Psalms— and those are overwhelmingly in Matthew's Gospel, which is directed to a Jewish audience. He quotes his own Scriptures very seldom in Mark, Luke, and John, which would seem to indicate that they each knew how to use the appropriate authority to suit each audience.

• Jesus *appears to ignore most of his own Bible, yet it clearly formed his whole consciousness.* That is the paradox. If we look at what he ignores, it includes any passages that appear to legitimate violence, imperialism, exclusion, purity, and dietary laws—of which there are many. These are the very ones we love to quote! Jesus is a *Biblically formed non-Bible quoter*, who gets the deeper stream, the spirit, the trajectory of his Jewish history and never settles for mere surface readings.

• When he does once quote Leviticus, he *quotes the one positive mandate* among long lists of negative ones: "You must love your neighbor as yourself" (see Leviticus 19:18). Yet we foolishly quote all the others when it is helpful to our case.

• He *openly disagrees with Scriptures that emphasize non-essentials and "mere human commandments"* that made their way into what are presented as divine commandments (see Mark 7:1–23 and almost all of Matthew 23).

◆ He *consistently and openly flaunts seemingly sacred taboos* like not working on the Sabbath, meeting with women, eating with sinners and non-Jews, not touching lepers, and purity codes in general. He is shamed and criticized for ignoring sacred ablutions; taboos against touching the dead, unclean people, and unclean foods; stoning of women adulterers; and many minor obligations that also seem silly to us, yet are clearly mandated in chapter and verse. Jesus has Jewish common sense and can never be called a legalist or a "conservative." In fact, he is accused of being a libertarian and a non-ascetic, instead of following the strict fasting of John the Baptist and his disciples (see Matthew 9:14). He is also hated for not washing his hands enough, which was an expected religious ritual (see Luke 11:38, for example).

◆ Jesus *is so simplistic and naive as to reduce the 613 clear Biblical commandments down to two:* love of God and love of neighbor (see Matthew 22:34–40). If I had talked the way

Jesus does to my seminary professors or early confessors, I would have been accused of being a reductionist or a situational ethicist—as, in fact, very conservative Catholics still do.

+ He *minimizes or even replaces commandments*, as when he tells the rich young man that it is all fine and good that he has obeyed the Ten Commandments, but what he really needs to do is sell everything and give the money to the poor (see Mark 10:21). From which worldview did this come? Yet, even then, he does not criticize the young man when he does not do it. In fact, he just "*looks steadily at him and loves him*"! How did we fail to notice the very thing that we all desire so much?

+ He *omits troublesome verses with which he does not agree*, as when he drops the final half verse from the Isaiah scroll when he first reads in the Nazareth synagogue (see Luke 4:18–19). But, as if to make the point, he "rolls up the scroll, hands it back to the attendant and sits down." We can imagine them glaring at him for adjusting the Scriptures to fulfill his own needs. They know the final line of Isaiah 61:2b is "to proclaim a day of vengeance from our God" and he ends with verse 2a, which "proclaims the Lord's day of favor." There he goes again, light and easy with the sacred text! Good Evangelicals would call that "selectively quoting" and pious Catholics would call it "cafeteria Catholicism"!

• Jesus frankly *uses Scripture in rather edgy ways to defend people*, like when he says that David went into the temple and took the loaves of offering to feed his troops (see Mark 2:26), or when he defends the poor man who works on the Sabbath to get his donkey out of a ditch (see Luke 14:5). His general principle seems to be summarized in his famous line that "the Sabbath was made for humanity, not humanity for the Sabbath" (see Mark 2:27). This sounds a lot like what many Christians would today call "mere humanism"! There is that dangerous "situation ethics" again!

• He *feels free to reinterpret the Law*—for example, when he says, six times in a row, "The Law says... but I say" in the Sermon on the Mount (see Matthew 5:21–48). The only reason his method probably does not bother us is that he is doing this with Jewish commandments. What if he were to use the same criteria with Christian practices, sacraments, or moral positions? We would be a lot more scandalized!

• He *consistently broadens the group toward greater inclusivity.* Well over sixty percent of Jesus' stories make the outsider the hero of the story, while criticizing the insider! Think of the most obvious Good Samaritan story, for one example (see Luke 10:25–37).

• He *introduces new, very memorable one-liners, not found previously in Scripture,* like, "I did not come for the healthy, but for sinners" or "the healthy do not need a doctor, but the sick do" (see Mark 2:17, Matthew 9:12,

60

and Luke 5:31). These often reveal his key, breakthrough ideas. Scholars are not sure whether they are unique to him or if he is quoting other sources, but he surely felt free to find wisdom outside the Biblical canon of his time. Evangelicals would call this secular humanism or "mere psychology."

• He is *not factually correct in some of his examples*, which clearly should suggest to people who like to pick apart arguments that this is not the point! For example, he describes the mustard seed as the smallest of all seeds and the mustard bush as the biggest of all shrubs in Matthew 13:32, which, in both cases, is not anywhere close to the truth. Is the Bible still to be called inerrant when Jesus uses erroneous examples to make spiritual points?

• Although I agree with him, he really *stretches it when he quotes Psalm 82:6* to assert that "you are all gods" in defending himself from leaders' accusations of blasphemy (see John 10:34). Few contemporary scholars would agree with this stretch as the intended meaning in Psalm 82, and most believers would call it a dangerous New Age aphorism. Yet it is put in the mouth of Jesus, and I would like to think I know exactly where he is going with it.

• Generally speaking, Jesus *makes use of his own Scriptures to teach a message of radical inclusivity, mercy, and justice,* and to negate the predominant religious messages of exclusion, religious righteousness, and oppression of the underdog, the impure, and the sinner. This is hard to deny from the Scriptural evidence, yet Christians will ignore the words of Jesus and find some Old Testament passage to make their point of necessary violence, exclusion of somebody, or justification of retributive justice. *When religion meets culture, culture wins, nine times out of ten!* Take that as normative. Many of our "culture wars" today hide behind religion and select Scriptures, while trusting in money, war, and power. Jesus gives the ego an almost perfect disguise—even from itself.

- Jesus clearly *considers "justice, mercy, and good faith" to be "the weightier matters the Law" (see* Matthew 23:23), and many statements such as this seem to indicate he did have a definite hierarchy of values. As Pope Francis has indicated, mercy is always right there at the top of Christian values! Not all Scriptures were created equal in Jesus' mind, which is a great blind spot for most fundamentalists, who have little or no skill or training in spiritual discernment. Jesus seems to teach that you can only tell goodness "by its fruits" (see Luke 6:43–45) and not just by the naked action itself. Paul then lists these fruits as "love, joy, peace, patience, kindness, goodness, trustfulness, gentleness, and self-control" (see Galatians 5:22–23). It is almost too simple and commonsensical, at least for a person who reads reality with body, mind, and spirit, rather than with the mind alone.

- Jesus *never punishes or shames any wrongdoers*; he only puts them back on their own conscience and tells them to take responsibility for their own actions, like the woman caught in adultery (see John 8:11). The only sinners with whom he is publicly upset are those who insist they are *not* sinners. Check me out on this. Jesus only excludes excluders and condemns condemners! Read, for example, almost all of Matthew 23.

SO HOW SHOULD YOU USE THE BIBLE?

At the risk of being simplistic, but for the sake of supporting you, and the many people who might not have the luxury of a solid or academic Scripture course (by far, most of humanity!), I would offer this spiritual advice so that you can interpret Scripture the way that Jesus did, and use it for good purposes.

• Offer a prayer for guidance from the Holy Spirit before you make your interpretation of an important text. Whether you are of the conservative or the liberal persuasion, this will *decenter your egoic need* to make the text say what you want or need it to say. Pray as long as it takes to get to this inner intellectual freedom and detachment.

• Once you have attained some honest degree of intellectual and emotional freedom, try to *move to a position of detachment* from your own will and its goals, needs, and desires. This might take some time, but without such freedom from your own control needs, you will invariably make a text say what you need and want it to say.

• Then you must *listen for a deeper voice than your own*, which you will know because it will never shame or frighten you, but rather strengthen you, *even when it is challenging you.* If it is God's voice, it will take away your illusions and your violence so completely and so naturally that you can barely identify with such previous feelings! I call this God's replacement therapy. *God does not ask and expect you to do anything new until God has first made it desirable and possible for you to do it.* Grace cannot easily operate under coercion, duress, shame, or guilt. Please trust me on this.

• If the interpretation leads your True Self to experience any or several of the fruits of the Spirit, as they are listed in Galatians 5:22–23—love, joy, peace, patience, kindness, goodness, trustfulness, gentleness, and self-control—I think you can trust this interpretation is from the Spirit, from the deeper stream of wisdom. *You can trust it even if it leads you to make a formal mistake.* With such goodwill, you will eventually see it as a mistake—and even that experience will draw you closer to divine union.

• If you sense any negative or punitive emotions like morose delight, feelings of superiority, self-satisfaction, arrogant dualistic certitude, desire for revenge, need for victory, or any spirit of dismissal or exclusion, you must trust that this is *not* the Jesus hermeneutic at work, but your own ego still steering the ship. Watch, especially, for any subtle feelings of righteousness or grabbing on to those taken-for-granted feelings of "I am right" and "they are wrong." It might even be a solid intellectual interpretation—but it will be spoiled by your impure use of it. *Christian virtue combination of both action and intention, and thus an art form more than a science.* This is precisely why a juridical, canonical approach to morality normally keeps you quite superficial.

♦ Finally, remember the temptation of Jesus in the desert (see Matthew 4:3–10). Three temptations to the misuse of power are listed—economic, religious, and political. Even Jesus must face these subtle disguises before he begins any public ministry. It is a warning to all of us. Our egoic power needs do not die easily.

Real evil is invariably good on one level or another, which is how politicians and devils have always been able to fool undiscerning people. It is precisely the partly good and partly bad that allows the ego to win out every time, because it only sees the part which is to its advantage—and thus sees it as "totally good." Then, the argument that most profits you is deemed "good" and the argument that threatens you is deemed "bad."

Only the humbled ego can see beyond this false dualism and choose the truly good—even when it also has some shadow sides to it. Holy persons are not afraid of carrying some shadow material (we all do, all the time, anyway), but purists want to imagine themselves above and beyond any complicity with evil whatsoever. This is the "parapet of the temple in the holy city" and "the high mountain from which he could see all the kingdoms of the world" (see Matthew 4:5, 8), where the last two temptations occur. Beware of such places! Instead, I return again and again to read a quote from St. Francis that hangs on my hermitage wall. He says a most dangerous but important thing: "We must bear patiently *not* being good…and not being *thought good*."⁹ That is heavy stuff. Only Thérèse of Lisieux (1873–1897) says the same so clearly.¹⁰ This is the testimony of two utterly free people.

Note also that the second—and religious—temptation has Satan quoting Scripture, and a pious and consoling Scripture at that: "He will put you in his angels' charge, and they will support you with their wings, lest you dash your foot against a stone" (see Psalm 91:11–12). Why would anyone question such a fine and courageous line from the Bible? Yet, Jesus says, in effect, "Do not play games with God" (see Matthew 4:7). He recognizes what T. S. Eliot (1888–1965) will later say so succinctly: "The last temptation is the greatest treason: to do the right deed for the wrong reason."¹¹

Just because you use Scripture, even in a God-affirming way, does not mean you are using Scripture for life and love, growth and wisdom—and for the sake of God or others.

Many of the worst genocides and atrocities in history have been supported by Scripture quotes in the mouths of selfish and scared people. Excessive God talk and quoting of Scripture are the best cover possible for a narcissistic personality. In fact, sometimes it seems to me that the churches that go on and on about "the greatness of God"—in both their sermons and their music—are often filled with the very groups and individuals that most want that greatness for themselves. I doubt if God needs us to be saying how great God is, as Satan does here with Jesus. Yes, religion is the best thing in the world and, also, the worst thing in the world—and so is Holy Scripture.

The corruption of the best is always the worst.

Only people who do not need to be powerful can handle spiritual power.

Only love can be entrusted with the Truth.

NOTES

1 Craig A. Evans, "The Scriptures of Jesus and His Earliest Followers," *The Canon Debate: On the Origins and Formation of the Bible,* ed. Lee Martin McDonald and James A. Sanders (Peabody, MA: Hendrickson, 2002), 191.

2 Emily Dickinson, *The Poems of Emily Dickinson: Reading Edition,* ed. R. W. Franklin (Cambridge, MA: Harvard University Press, 1998), 494.

3 Parker Palmer, *On the Brink of Everything: Grace, Gravity, and Getting Old* (Oakland, CA: Berrett-Koehler, 2018), 57.

4 For more on this, see Richard Rohr, *Immortal Diamond: The Search for Our True Self* (San Francisco, CA: Jossey-Bass, 2013).

5 For more on this, see Richard Rohr, *The Universal Christ: How a Forgotten Reality*

Changes Everything You See, Hope for, and Believe (New York: Convergent, forthcoming).

6 Richard Rohr and Andreas Ebert, *The Enneagram: A Christian Perspective*, trans. Peter Heinegg (New York: Crossroad, 2016).

7 Rohr, *The Universal Christ.*

8 William McNamara, as quoted by Walter J. Burghardt, "Contemplation: A Long, Loving Look at the Real," *Church,* No. 5 (Winter 1989), 14–17.

9 Thomas of Celano, "Second Life of St. Francis," *St. Francis of Assisi: Omnibus of Sources,* ed. Marion Habig (Cincinnati, OH: Franciscan Media, 2009), 481–482.

10 "If you are willing to serenely bear the trial of being displeasing to yourself, then you will be for Jesus a pleasant place of shelter," in *Collected Letters of Saint Thérèse of Lisieux,* ed. Abbe Combes, trans. F. J. Sheed (New York: Sheed and Ward, 1949), 303.

11 T. S. Eliot, *Murder in the Cathedral* (New York: Houghton Mifflin Harcourt, 1935, 1963), 44. Used with permission.